CONTENT MARKETING

INSIDER'S SECRET TO ONLINE SALES & LEAD GENERATION

RICK RAMOS

One Night Expert Publishing

Published by One Night Expert Publishing

New York, New York 10001

This publication is designed to provide accurate and
authoritative information in regard to the subject matter
covered. It is sold with the understanding that the publisher
is not engaged in rendering legal, accounting, or other
professional service. If legal advice or other expert assistance
is required, the services of a competent professional person
should be sought.

Questions for the author?

rick@rickramos.com

www.rickramos.com

PRAISE FOR
CONTENT MARKETING
INSIDER'S SECRET TO ONLINE SALES & LEAD GENERATION

"A must-read for anyone wanting to learn about the awesome power of content marketing and how it can transform your business. Full of wonderful and inspiring case studies from some of the top brands in the world! This book will save you from months of research and give you and your team the knowledge you need to create a successful content marketing playbook."

Jim F. Kukral, Author of the top selling book "Attention!"

"Content marketing is the only way to become a true thought leader. This book provides all the fundamentals of how to think about, generate, distribute, and measure the results of great content.

There is no substitute for a well-executed content marketing strategy, especially for B2B and SAAS businesses. Rick spells out everything you need to build a great content foundation."

Peter Hamilton, CEO of HasOffers.com

"Rick has created a concise, step-by-step guide for marketers that explains how brands can create and leverage content to increase leads and generate sales. A must-read for any marketer navigating today's content-fueled media landscape."

Steve Hall, Adrants.com - Editor and Publisher

"Thinking about adding content marketing to your strategy? Want to know the best way to market your business? You need to read this book!

Rick Ramos explains in simple terms why every company should incorporate these strategies to get ahead. He unravels the magic of content marketing and gives you a clear roadmap on how to drive sales and leads from your website."

Scott Lynn, Founder and Chairman of Adknowledge.com

"This book is about more than just content marketing. It's about making your business become a part of the conversation. Through this book you learn how to inform your customers to make intelligent decisions. I think that every business should adopt the strategies that it outlines."

Clark Landry, Co-founder and Chairman at SHIFT.com

"People many times approach Internet marketing from a technical angle but it's really about people. Rick Ramos, in this book, breaks down using content to help market your business while helping to engage and educate your future customers. You'll learn how to become a "thought leader" in your space and become a leader. These approaches are easy to implement by anyone with the desire, from a Forture 500 company to a single person startup."

Dan Obegi, CEO of DermStore.com

ABOUT THE AUTHOR

Mr. Rick Ramos is a seasoned veteran in online marketing with over seventeen year's experience developing global brands for major industry players, including his time spent working at a comScore-rated top 50 web property and two of the world's largest ad networks as Vice President of Marketing.

Rick develops and builds online media strategies for companies of all sizes, including several Fortune 500 companies. He has been quoted in and his companies profiled by CNBC Business, The Wall Street Journal, AMEX OpenForum, Portfolio, Law.com, Ars Technica, CBS MoneyWatch, and more.

Rick also created the number one most-viewed banner of all time with over 3 billion impressions worldwide.

CONTENTS

"I don't know the rules of grammar ... If you're trying to persuade people to do something, or buy something, it seems to me you should use their language, the language they use every day, the language in which they think. We try to write in the vernacular."

David Ogilvy
Father of Modern Advertising

DEDICATION

This book is dedicated first to my mother and father.

This book would not have been possible without their love and support.

I would also like to thank Stephanie Lichtenstein and the team at MicroMediaMarketing. com for all the information regarding social media.

Lastly, I would like to thank my godfather, Tony, who came into this country without a penny, graduated with honors from Yale Medical School on a full scholarship, and became a successful doctor. He taught me that with hard work and dedication you can do anything in life.

INTRODUCTION

Back in the late 90's, I created one of the most viewed online banners of all time, with over 3 billion impressions worldwide. It also had one of the highest click-through rates in the industry, and people where happy to engage with it. Boy... have times changed!

It has been documented that people these days just ignore traditional banners. Click-through rates have dropped drastically, and online businesses have been looking for new methods to grab your attention. The problem is that the Internet has changed how people discover and shop for things. People do research on Google, find out what their friends think on Facebook and browse possibilities on Pinterest.

So, you might be asking, "How does a business get attention these days?" The answer is: content marketing!

The great thing about content marketing is that businesses big and small can get started and become part of the conversation. They can make true connections with people and, more importantly, drive sales and leads for their products and services.

Anyone can get started without spending a penny, and great content produces long-term results. I've known people that have written articles years ago that are still bringing in tons of business. The only thing you need is commitment and drive.

PART I
CONTENT MARKETING EXPOSED

1 WHAT IS CONTENT MARKETING?

Content marketing is a marketing technique that uses high-quality, relevant content to educate, engage, and acquire your target customer. Content marketing isn't just creating content for the sake of producing content; your objective is always sales. The true potential of content marketing lies in its ability to provide a conversion path for your leads to follow—on their own schedule and at their convenience.

Content marketing succeeds when you provide your prospect with educational information and context about your products or services, minus a sales pitch. It's the opposite of outbound marketing; your goal is to educate. There are neither direct sales pitches nor calls to action; what you are really trying to do is create influence. Content marketing can consist of a wide variety of media: text, photos, audio, video, etc.

Content Marketing is a pull versus push strategy. Your content should engage and attract people; it's not meant to interrupt someone's conscious thought. Many people mistakenly confuse social media for content marketing. This is understandable, but think of social media as just one channel in a content marketing strategy.

The five components that define content marketing are:

1. Editorial – It's a biased opinion piece created by someone. Content marketing isn't an impartial news piece; it's created to get key messaging points

across to the user.

2. Marketing – This might be stating the obvious, but your goal is to market your product or service. You might try to do it in an entertaining way, but your ultimate goal is to—in the end—sell your product.

3. Influential – Your ultimate goal is to have a have a powerful effect on people and what they think and do. You want them to think of you as a thought leader in a field or industry.

4. Multi-Channel – You don't create content to be on an isolated island. Once you create content, you want to spread it everywhere. You can start by posting something on your corporate blog, and you then might post excerpts on Facebook, Twitter, etc., to drive traffic to your blog page. If your content contains some interesting facts about your company or industry, you might shoot an e-mail over to a reporter you know in your industry. You'll also want to make sure the content you posted is search-engine friendly so that people can find it through Google.

5. Targeted – You want to create content that will appeal to your typical customers. If you're a women's jewelry designer, you're not going to cover the latest release of the Ford F150 pickup truck. Instead, you'll probably want to cover lifestyle, beauty, and other topics that interest your overall audience. If you run the marketing for Apple iPhone developer relations, you might want to cover the latest in programming and app marketing techniques.

2 WHY CONTENT MARKETING?

Sometimes people have the mistaken belief that content marketing is free, but as the old saying goes, time is money. An all-encompassing content-marketing strategy requires a bit of work in both content creation and distribution. You can begin a content-marketing strategy as just a single entrepreneur working part-time on content or as a team of writers, social media managers, SEO experts, and more with full-time salaries.

So why are more people putting an average of 25 percent or more of their marketing budget into content marketing? Because it works and it allows you to talk directly to your customers without a middleman filtering your message.

You see, today's consumer sees an average of 5,000 advertisers a day[1], very few of which are relevant to him or her. At the same time, during the course of the year, most people are in the market for tons of products and services and actively research the issues, solutions, and providers of interest to them. Content marketing addresses the prospect's keen interest in detailed information.

Content marketing puts the prospect in charge of the initial stages of the sales cycle, learning about your company's approach to the market or problem that needs addressing. Although prospects are reluctant to initiate a conversation with a sales representative too early in the sales cycle, content marketing ensures that their interest remains high—on their own terms.

And the numbers bear this out: Seven out of ten consumers say they prefer to learn about companies and solution providers by reading articles or viewing videos over traditional, outbound marketing, which many deem "disruptive." More than three-quarters of these consumers understand that content marketing seeks to promote a product point of view, but they see the value in having insight information and context about the product. Two-thirds feel it helps them make better purchasing decisions.[2]

Given the consumer's embrace of content marketing, it's no surprise that marketers now spend over a quarter of their marketing budget on content marketing.[3] B2B companies that pay attention to content—via blogs and other efforts—generate 67 percent more leads per month on average.[4] And the number of leads rise substantially when companies use content ad networks to amplify this work.

Some of you might ask, will content marketing replace advertising? The answer is no. Content marketing should be an important part of your marketing mix. Your company should have a blend of both inbound and outbound marketing efforts. These combined efforts are greater than any one specific strategy.

Share of Average Time Spent per Day with Select Media by US Adults vs. US Ad Spending Share, 2011
% of total

TV

42.5%

42.2%

Internet*

25.9%

21.9%

Radio

14.6%

10.9%

Mobile

10.1%

0.9%

Newspapers

4.0%

15.0%

Magazines

2.8%

9.7%

■ Time spent share   ■ Ad spending share

Note: *time spent with the internet excludes internet access via mobile, but online ad spending includes mobile internet ad spending; due to this, the total of the ad spending shares for all the media adds up to more than 100%
Source: eMarketer, Dec 2011

134682   www.eMarketer.com

Figure 1 – Advertisers are still chasing old media methods and are spending money where the users aren't. As this figure shows, there is still a lot of opportunity in the Internet and a huge gap in mobile spend.

The top four reasons that businesses are moving to content marketing:

1. **Consumer attitudes are changing toward traditional media** – In today's world, people turn first to the Internet to conduct their buying research and decisions. They are becoming more knowledgeable consumers and crave more information. They aren't sitting around waiting for you to interrupt what they are doing with your marketing message. They have DVRs and

ad-blockers and they have learned to tune out advertising. Basically, they no longer want to be sold; they want to be educated and make informed decisions. If you're providing that content, you can lead the conversation.

"If it's called the USA Today, why is all the news from yesterday? BAM. Busted!"
- **Stephen Colbert**

Additionally, consumers are presently turning away from traditional, big media sources. They no longer wait for old news to be edited and presented to them; they want updated, real-time information. According to comScore, the top three web properties are search engines and number four is Facebook, the leading social media property. The good thing for content marketers is that sites like Google allow anyone to rank for specific search terms that present great written content. The same holds true for social media; the old gatekeepers are gone and good content rises democratically.

Table 3

comScore Top 50 Properties (U.S.)
December 2012
Total U.S. – Home, Work and University Locations
Source: comScore Media Metrix

Rank	Property	Unique Visitors (000)
	Total Internet : Total Audience	*221,486*
1	Google Sites	191,363
2	Yahoo! Sites	184,935
3	Microsoft Sites	168,889
4	FACEBOOK.COM	149,602
5	Amazon Sites	120,810
6	AOL, Inc.	110,139
7	Glam Media	109,734
8	Ask Network	104,080
9	Wikimedia Foundation Sites	85,847
10	Apple Inc.	83,609

2. **You can't count on traditional media to help you reach your customers** – In the past, if you were a business, you could get a little press and place a weekly ad in the newspaper or magazines to reach your target customer. This worked both locally and nationally. These days, according to the Newspaper Association of America (NAA. org), only 29 percent of US adults ages 18-34 turn to newspaper print and online editions. Also, according to the Audit Bureau of Circulations which works with magazine publishers, circulation has dropped an average of 1-2 percent every year for the last five years. Marketers are beginning to see that all content is starting to shift online and the ivory towers of big media can no longer be counted on to reach consumers.

3. **Content quality is going down for traditional media** – The traditional media empires are in a state of decay; there is a new report every month of another newspaper laying off reporters. To compensate, newspapers are turning more and more to news services such as the Associated Press for content. They are all starting to publish the same exact content because it's cheaper than writing original content.

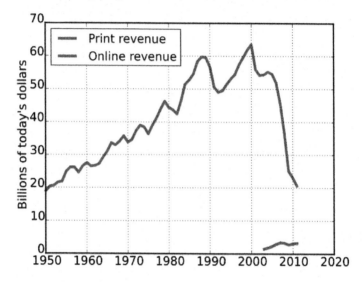

See an opportunity? With all these layoffs and budget reductions, newspapers are producing less quality content. There is a void in the marketplace for quality content on a wide variety of subjects. Your high quality content can fill this void and educate customers.

4. **It's never been easier or cheaper to produce great content** – With the continuing evolution of the

web, it's become cheaper and cheaper every year to produce and disseminate content. Free tools like WordPress can allow a single entrepreneur to produce a website that would have taken a team of 10 people to maintain 10 years ago. Social media now allows a small business to maintain constant communication with their local customers and publicize specials and time-sensitive information. Sites like Elance.com, TeamLauncher.com, and oDesk.com allow people to hire both freelancers and full-time employees to work from any location from around the world.

Featured Company EXAMPLE – LEGO Club

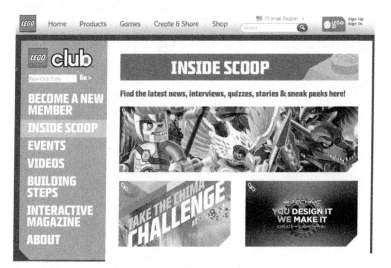

LEGO, the popular line of construction toys, started in Denmark in 1949. Everyone remembers playing with LEGOs as a child, but the company began running into trouble in the 80s when their patent ran out:

"In the 1980s and 1990s, LEGO faced a tremendous threat from competing construction toys. After all, the very simplicity of LEGO's building blocks also made them very easy to duplicate, both by small-scale copycats as well as established toy companies. LEGO unsuccessfully tried to block Tyco Toys, Inc., from selling the Super Blocks series after LEGO's patent ran out in 1983. The company knew it needed to build a powerhouse brand and integrated marketing approach to compete against a growing set of building-block imitators," said a company spokesman.

These days LEGO works more like a media company than a traditional toy company. LEGO club is just one of hundreds of content initiates the company produces every year. They produce a free magazine, online videos, microsites, events, and more. On Facebook they have almost four million fans that interact with the brand every day.

3 WHOSE JOB IS CONTENT MARKETING?

The main problem with defining who is in charge with content marketing is that it sometimes overlaps with different departments within a large organization (e.g., marketing, PR, search engine optimization managers, CMS/IT involvement, and more). You'll see some people claim "everyone" is responsible for creating content within an organization, but in reality it rarely works that way.

Companies are unique in that you'll have different levels of buy-in from senior management, and they will place content in different places within an organizational chart. Usually, it flows more smoothly when one person or department is in charge of managing content marketing even if it's not in an "official" capacity.

Some job titles for those in charge of content marketing can include the following:

- Chief / VP of Content

- CMO / VP of Marketing

- Editor

- Chief Blogger

- Community Manager

- Social Media Manager

- PR Manager

We'll discuss content strategy in more depth later on within this book, but for now think of who in your organization would be the best fit to handle the management of content marketing. What are your internal human resources for handling the production of content? You have many different types of content that can be produced—text, audio, video, etc. Are some people better suited to one type of content versus another?

PART II
FINDING YOUR VOICE

1 WHO IS YOUR TARGET CUSTOMER?

One of the first things you need to do before writing any content is identify the audience for whom you're creating it. This will help you to not only figure out what topics to cover but also what form of content will best reach this audience (video, pictures, etc.). To uncover this information, you need to create a user profile and persona. A profile describes the overall characteristics of the target audience while personas are more like illustrations of virtual users; they are created based on data collected from user research on real users. More importantly, however, personas represent behavior patterns and motivations.

User Profile – User profiles are based on a list of characterizations about your users, and each business might have a different list that is important to them. You can get lots of this data from a variety of sources: your customer list, website analytics, Facebook Insights page, etc. The following is a short list of some broad characteristics you can use to identify your customers, but each business is different and other characteristics might be important:

- Age

- Gender

- Location

- Language

- Culture

- Computer Skill

- Disabilities

- Income

User Persona – A persona is a fictional character created to represent the different types that typically use your product or service. Creating personas is useful in helping you consider the goals, behaviors, and desires of your customers, and they help guide you in the creation of content. Personas are typically created from data gathered during interviews with your existing customer base.

You can create a simple, one-page description that includes their goals, attitudes, skills, and behavioral patterns with a few fictional personal details to make the character come alive. Companies will usually make a few different personas for each product within their product line. One persona is usually considered the primary persona for each given product. Adding a human face to your customers usually makes it easier to write and produce content for them and gives everyone in your organization a better understanding of your target customer.

Here are a few examples of personas:

- Matthew is 51-year-old married father with three children and one grandchild. He has a doctorate in agricultural economics and spends his work time requesting and reviewing research reports, preparing memos and briefs for agency heads, and supervising staff efforts in food safety and inspection. He is focused and goal-oriented within a strong leadership role. One of his concerns is maintaining the quality of the output across all programs. He is comfortable using a computer and refers to himself as an intermediate Internet user. He is connected via a T1 connection at work and dial-up at home. He uses e-mail extensively and uses the web about 1.5 hours during his work day. He is most likely heard saying: "Can you get me that staff analysis by Tuesday?" – Actual persona developed by the US Department of Agriculture's (USDA) Economic Research Service (ERS)

- Lisa is a 27-year-old single ad exec who has been using the Internet for the last 10 years. She uses her Macbook, iPad, or iPhone phone to access the web—whatever is close at hand. She can be impulsive and make quick decisions but usually takes a few minutes to research important purchases. She lives with a roommate in a two-bedroom apartment and reviews dailycandy.com every day to see what's hot. She's been using an online dating website lately but rarely goes out with anyone she speaks with on the site.

- Mark is 36 years old and works for an e-commerce company in IT. He is well educated and got his master's degree online after working for a few years out of college. He is recently engaged to a girl he's been dating for three years and will be searching for a new house shortly. He loves buying everything online—including toilet paper—and hates to go to stores. He drinks only niche microbrews and spends 10 hours a month playing video games.

2 TYPES OF CONTENT

Teaching about your product or service

One of the basic pillars of effective content marketing is teaching about your product or service. Your product can range from the simple to the complex to understand. Regardless of where your product falls on the scale, producing content that teaches consumers about your product is an amazing way to get people to understand and buy your product or service.

If you are selling a complex product or service to other businesses, try and take into account all the people from different departments that will be involved in the decision process. As an example, imagine you're selling online recruiting software. It's obvious that the human resources department will be using this software, but take into account that every department in the company might also be using this software in a more limited capacity. Think about how you might explain this software to all the different departments that might use this software.

Simple Products	Complex Products
Razors	Appliance Repair
Paper Towels	Enterprise Software
Blenders	Financial Services

Regardless of where you fall on the scale of complexity, try and figure out how you can educate the consumer about your product.

EXAMPLE - Mint.com – Financial Services

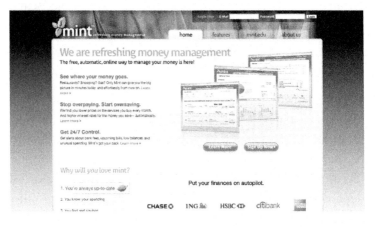

Mint.com launched in 2006 in the highly competitive personal finances space competing with established services like Quicken. Within three years, the company became the market leader in online personal finance and sold to Intuit for $170 million. They owe much of their success to a well-executed content marketing strategy. Mint.com viewed their corporate blog almost like one of the larger personal finance magazines. This startup staffed their blog with a full-time editorial staff and heavily used freelance contributors.

They began investing time in social media channels including Facebook, Reddit, Digg, and more. After months of offering consistent, high quality content, Mint.com started to establish trust within these communities—trust in their content but also trust in their company. Many of these users quickly became customers and even began spreading the gospel of using Mint.com to control your finances.

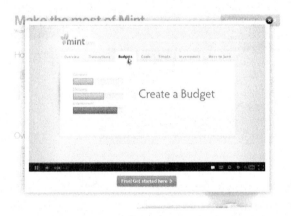

They used a combination of videos, infographics, slideshows, news, tips, and more. They made sure everything was easy to understand for people with limited education in finance.

The following are some of the elements that lead to Mint. com's success:

- Dedicate human resources to create content

- Enforce high quality editorial standards on content

- Use social channels to share content and encourage virality

- Dedication and patience in building up an audience

- Complete buy-in from senior management

EXAMPLE – PartSelect.com

PartSelect.com, launched in 1999, has been a leader in helping do-it-yourselfers with their home repair needs by providing repair parts and the know-how to fix their household appliances and consumer electronics. Their commitment to content marketing has lead to a huge selection of articles on repairing your own appliances and over 600 videos that have garnered almost 6 million views.

One of the key differentiators between PartSelect.com and others in their space is their willingness to answer each and every question—even if it's already posted on their YouTube page, Facebook, Twitter, wherever. These can sometimes be pretty technical questions, but they take the time to answer each and every one. It's easy to see why people trust the company and purchase their products from them.

Repairing an appliance isn't something people do often. I personally had a small part on a refrigerator break and learned about PartSelect.com from my own research on how to replace it. Following the instructions, I learned it was a simple procedure, and it allowed me to save time and money.

Entertainment Content

Making your customers laugh, sing along with joy, and touching their hearts is an amazing way to connect your brand with your customers. Nothing tears down our guard faster than experiencing an emotion through some form of content. People don't remember facts and figures, but they do remember a great story and they love to share those stories with friends.

There are many ways to entertain while selling at the same time. The use of videos, pictures, and sounds allow you to connect with your customers in a very different and emotional way from many other types of content. Remember to think about your audience and try and figure out what's most important in their lives. Use social media to discover their likes and preferences and try to match them.

EXAMPLE – DollarShaveClub.com

This e-commerce startup launched in 2012 and quickly developed a following selling razors that are delivered monthly on a subscription basis. Its first video is hilarious. It was uploaded to YouTube and features their CEO Michael Dubin talking about their razors while riding a forklift and packing boxes with a guy in a bear suit. He goes on and declares, "Our blades are f**ing great." The Santa Monica, Calif., company doesn't disclose the number of customers it has, but it did say that 12,000 people signed up in the first 48 hours after it launched its first video that went viral. Over 9 million people have seen their video to date. Not every CEO has Mr. Dubin's sense of comedic timing, but if you do, you should think about using humor while selling your product.

EXAMPLE – Blendtec / Will It Blend?

Blendtec is the king of video content marketing with their "Will it blend?" video series. This company began in 1975 and made some of the best blenders on the market. It's amazing to think this utility product that's already in almost everyone's home became the shining example of video content marketing. Tom Dickson, the inventor of the blender, always loved demonstrating the power of his blender to anyone that would pass by. When he put on a demonstration with his blender chopping up a piece of wood, he realized people would always stop to stare.

He got the idea to get a $20 lab coat and some goggles and to start blending different items. He's blended golf balls, lighters, even a crowbar. His most popular video (with over 15 million views) is him blending an iPad in the blender. These funny videos have received over 200 million views and increased sales for the company over 700 percent.

Utilities and Apps

When people first think of content marketing, they think of blog posts, videos, and funny pictures. Another great approach is providing tools and utilities to your clients; it's an easy way to get them to visit your site when they need your product the most.

A classic example is a bank offering a mortgage calculator on its site. This allows consumers to figure out what their mortgage payment would be on a house but it also allows banks to brand themselves when someone is early in the mortgage process. These days people aren't always on their computers, so offering a free mobile application of the same tool is a great way to reach out to consumers.

This Zillow mortgage calculator is the first one that comes up in the Apple App store. It's well done and has great reviews from almost 350 people.

Every industry is different but try and think about the tools that your clients use to make their decisions. Try to provide these tools and get involved in their decision-making process early.

EXAMPLE – MaryKay.com / Virtual Makeover

For 50 years, Mary Kay has worked in the beauty industry. They have 2.5 million Mary Kay Independent Beauty Consultants around the globe, and they do $3 billion in global annual wholesale sales. Mary Kay is one of the top beauty brands and is a direct seller in more than 35 markets around the world. They also use content marketing to help sell and educate their consultants and customers.

Their virtual online makeover tool allows people to upload their own photo (or use a default model) and apply different colors of lipstick, eye shadow, blush, and more to see what Mary Kay product looks best on them. They have taken the same strategy that department stores have used for years and brought it online in a fun and easy way.

EXAMPLE – Geico

GEICO is the third-largest private passenger auto insurance company in the United States. They provide millions of auto insurance quotes to US drivers annually and they do most of them online. They are firm believers in content marketing and have the typical assortment of financial calculators and tools on their website. One of the interesting things that Geico has done is they created games and entertainment apps based on characters from their commercials. These apps are fun and silly but they help position a boring product (sorry Geico) into something people can relate to and with which they can interact.

Content Curation

Nearly 95 percent of marketers doing content marketing now use some form of content aggregation according to the Content Curation Adoption Survey 2012. This involves the process of constantly finding, organizing, and sharing highly relevant content that caters to your audience. Of those surveyed, 85 percent believe this helps establish them as thought leaders within their industry.

Most content aggregators blend company-generated materials with third-party content. Social media channels are important for all content aggregators as 79 percent use social media to find new sources of content and about the same number of people use it to distribute that content.

You can start off by using a few simple tools that make finding content easier.

1. **Newsfeeds**: RSS feeds are one of the easiest ways to receive targeted content from a specific website. Some very large sites also have individual RSS

feeds for categories within their site.

2. **Google Alerts:** http://www.google.com/alerts allows you to set up search terms that will automatically run at selected intervals that search news sources throughout the web.

3. **Google Blog Search:** http://www.google.com/blogsearch allows you to search a large number of blogs and maybe find a few new ones. You can have Google Alerts search blogs as well, but you can use this at times when you are looking for new blogs you might want to add to an RSS feed.

4. **All Top:** http://alltop.com imports the stories from the top news websites and blogs for any given topic and displays the headlines of the five most recent stories. It's a good place to see what's going on at a glance on a certain topic.

5. **Social Media:** There are a ton of people and companies in your industry on Facebook, LinkedIn, Twitter, and more that share great stories about a variety of topics. These people are also a good source for news.

EXAMPLE - The Small Cell Hub

The Small Cell Hub is a portal for all news, opinions, and events relating to small cellular towers. These small cells are low-power wireless access points that operate in a licensed spectrum, are operator-managed, and feature edge-based intelligence. This exciting new class of product promises to improve the mobile experience for people using mobile devices in residential, enterprise, and public-access environments.

The Small Cell Hub is operated by the Small Cell Forum using software by Curata. The Small Cell Forum is a not-for-profit membership organization founded in 2007 to enable and promote small cell technology worldwide. It's a small niche publication but it's valuable to its membership.

EXAMPLE – Disney

Walt Disney Parks and Resorts began curating user-generated content in its new "Let the Memories Begin" campaign. They allowed visitors to submit photos and videos from visits to the resort. This allows users to share their experience with others and gives Disney a never-ending supply of content for their site with real stories from real people.

Disney actually began using this user-submitted content in TV spots for the theme parks. The commercials are touching and more real than actors playing a role in a Disney park.

Disney will take the concept further by incorporating family photos into its theme parks with its "Let the Memories Begin" nighttime show. In Orlando, guest photos will be projected on Cinderella's Castle in the Magic Kingdom. In California, the backdrop will be the "It's a Small World" ride.

Disney is a company built on knowing how to create emotional connections and telling a good story. The best stories are sometimes your customers' stories; think about how you can help to facilitate the sharing of those stories.

PART III
CONTENT CHANNELS

1 CORPORATE WEBSITE

Your corporate website should be the backbone of your content marketing strategy. When possible, you should always strive to drive traffic to your own personal website. To do this, you should always keep it alive with fresh content. These days, updating a website isn't as difficult as it was even five years ago. With the advent of content management systems (CMS) like WordPress, it's very easy to update a website on a daily basis.

Company Blog

A blog is a type of website or part of a website that is usually arranged in chronological order from the most recent "post" (or story) at the top of the main page to the older entries toward the bottom. A blog can be written by a single person (sometimes called a blogger) or a team of people and should be updated frequently. Blogs generally cover a single topic and, in the case of a corporate blog, a company or industry. The obscure topics of some blogs would amaze you.

Typically, when you visit a blog, you are shown only the latest stories and you might not realize the huge archive of past articles that it contains. Over time these archives can be quite large if you've been a busy blogger. They can also be a great source to continue generating traffic from search engines.

One of the things you need to decide when creating a blog is if you're going to allow comments on your posts. There can be both pros and cons to allowing comments. By allowing them, you can help to generate a sense of community on your website. The con is that they need to be monitored on a continual basis to make sure that the comments align with your corporate goals. Usually, this is something that needs to be discussed internally and may depend on your industry. Blog posts can be anything from a long article about the state of your industry to photos from the company Christmas party. The one thing I would say about blogs though is if you're going to set up a blog, make sure you're going to commit to writing on a schedule. There is nothing worse than going to a corporate blog whose last entry was in 1999.

White Papers & E-books

A white paper is a report or guide that helps readers understand a particulate topic. Typically, B2B marketers use them as a sales tool. They can contain research findings, survey results, or tips about an issue, and they can feature particular products or services from a vendor. Most of the time, users are required to register their e-mail to receive a particular white paper, and the user can be sent additional marketing materials.

The three most popular types of white papers are:

- **Backgrounder**: These typically describe the technical and/or business benefits for your product or service. They are good tools to use to explain an unfamiliar or misunderstood product to your audience.

- **Numbered list:** These are the fastest and easiest type of white paper to create. They are easy reads that provide a simple overview of a topic. You also use them to introduce FUD (fear, uncertainty, and doubt) into an industry marketplace (e.g., "Ten Questions to Ask Before You Buy XXXX").

- **Problem/solution:** These are often the ones that generate the most leads at the top of a sales funnel. They describe a problem within your industry that went unsolved until your product or service was released. They use facts, figures, and logic to promote your new solution.

E-books are book-length publications in digital form. Many times the term "e-book" is used in place of "white paper" for the same style of document from a content marketing perspective. E-books can be pretty much of any length, from 10 to 300 pages or more. When using them for content marketing, most people keep them on the shorter side.

Podcasts

A podcast is an episodic program delivered through the Internet. They can consist of audio, video, text, or a combination of the three. The term is a blend of "broadcast" and "iPod" as podcasts became extremely popular with Apple's release of the iPod. Applications such as iTunes make downloading and subscribing to podcasts fast and easy. Downloading the latest release becomes an automatic process through these tools and makes it a great way to automatically distribute your message to your customers on a continuous basis.

EXAMPLE – Novell's SalesTalk podcast is continuing training for their third-party sales partners. It keeps them up-to-date with the latest products and technology releases.

Corporate Videos & Webinars

"Corporate videos" is a general term to describe a video used as a business tool rather than entertainment. There are many reasons to produce a corporate video, but they usually fall within two camps:

- **Training** – Video is a great medium to educate people about your product, service, or the state of your industry. Many highly technical products are easier to understand when presented in video rather than just an article or in audio. You might want to train your customers or third parties that sell and service your product or service. You might also be surprised that many people will go through your training videos before they purchase your product or service, turning it into a sales tool.

EXAMPLE – MailChimp has excellent training videos that are available to view even if you're not a paying subscriber. These become valuable selling tools to heavy tire kickers that don't want to speak with a salesperson and want to educate themselves.

- **Marketing & Promotional Videos** – Today, most videos are made for online distribution through websites, video-sharing sites, and social networks. Videos can be something as simple as you explaining your online software with screen capture software, using a webcam to record yourself talking, to a full-blown production with cast and crew.

EXAMPLE – Google Project Glass is a research and development program created by Google to develop an augmented reality head-mounted display. They developed a video to demonstrate how the product would function in the real world. This video has been viewed almost 20 million times and helped get developers interested in the project. Time magazine already named it one of the "Best Inventions of the Year 2012" and the product isn't even available to the public yet.

Webinars are a combination of the words "web" and "seminar" and are video presentations, lectures, or workshops that are transmitted over the web. The key feature of a webinar is its interactive elements. Users have the ability to give and receive feedback on the presentation. This interaction makes them slightly different from other forms of video. Many people record these webinars as well and make them available to view after the event has taken place.

E-mail and Newsletters

E-mail and newsletters have been the granddaddy of content marketing for a long time. Many companies that don't even have blogs will send out the occasional newsletter or update. Usually, with e-mail, you want to have a limited amount of content with a call to action to drive the user to your website.

Developing your e-mail list through your website is of upmost importance. It allows you to have an ongoing relationship with your potential or existing customers and keep them updated on your products or services. Remember, you can also segment your e-mail list in all sorts of different ways and send custom-targeted e-mails to your different audiences.

There is a wide variety of inexpensive services that will allow any company to send out e-mails quickly and easily. The two leaders in the space are ConstantContact.com and MailChimp.com. They offer starter plans for free, so there is little reason not to try adding e-mail to your content marketing strategy.

Case Studies

Case studies are very effective marketing tools for all businesses. They highlight a satisfied customer that uses your product or service in a positive, real-world scenario. They're usually is only a page or two in a narrative form and clearly illustrate a problem and a solution with a testimonial and a light amount of data or charts to easily demonstrate the effectiveness of your product or service at a glance.

Many companies these days are now doing video case studies on their clients. These are admittedly a bit harder to do because you need to get your client physically involved, but they are more powerful than a standard text-based case study because your client delivers the message directly. SalesForce.com has done an outstanding job in doing video case studies on their clients. They even allow their clients to submit their stories on their website to share with the community.

Online Training

Many products and services are complex to use and have a steep learning curve. Online training and education is a great way to explain these products and services in video, text, and self-paced tutorials.

AdWords is Google's advertising product where people can by text ads on Google next to search results. It can be a fairly complex product to use, and Google has done a great job making free, extensive training available to anyone. You don't even need to be an existing advertiser; all videos are available to the public.

All this content helps educate people both pre- and post-sale. Many people are cautious and want to fully learn about and understand a product before committing to it.

Customer Service

In a lot of ways, customer service IS content marketing. You're trying to serve your customers all the information they need regardless of where they are within the sales cycle. You're trying to educate them and get them to either make a purchase or remain a customer. Your customer service strategy will fall under two different approaches: proactive and reactive.

Proactive Customer Service – With a proactive approach, you are trying to anticipate the needs of your customers. You are trying to provide them with as much information as you can about your product so that they can educate themselves and solve their own customer service issues without having to contact your company. Many people would rather head over to your website than pick up the phone and call your company.

One company that does proactive customer service right is GE's appliance division. In the major appliances category, the ASCI survey has named General Electric number one in customer service. They anticipate the potential problems and questions their customers might have with an appliance and offer solutions and information online.

They provide access to:

- Downloadable Product Manuals

- Installation Instructions

- FAQ – List of Frequently Asked Questions

- Knowledge Base – A huge searchable database with information on all products and services provided by the company

- Maintenance and Troubleshooting Videos

- Common Parts and Accessories Information

- Register a Product

- Schedule a Service Call

- Recall Information

- Contact Information – Phone & E-mail

- Links to Social Media Pages

Reactive Customer Service – Many times customers do not want to spend time reading the available customer service information and will want to communicate with you directly. The Internet is a wide-open place, and if you don't give your customers open avenues of communication, they will hold the conversation elsewhere on the web. There are many different avenues available for communication, either public or private, that you can choose to support. Here are just a few of the available options:

- "Contact Us" form on your website

- Voice & E-mail

- Website chat – Tools such as snapengage.com allow you to easily add both inbound and proactive chat to your website.

- Community Forums – Forums are a great way to provide customer service in an open and public way. This also allows others to view previous support occurrences. Many companies also find community members will sometimes help and answer each other's questions.

- Twitter, Facebook and other Social Media Options – People these days expect companies to provide customer service through social media. Many companies develop customer services teams that specifically monitor and help support customers on social channels.

EXAMPLE – JetBlue

Here's an example of JetBlue having conversations with

individuals publicly using Twitter. They are updating users on a pending storm and sharing links that can be useful to others.

They will even address negative comments by users.

This not only addresses the single complaint, but it also shows that JetBlue is proactive and cares about their customers.

2 SOCIAL NETWORKS

When we talk about "social networks" in this book, we are referring to an online service like Facebook that focuses on building social connections between people and companies. Most social networks were originally web-based, but mobile use has exploded recently and will continue to grow. In 2013, over 70 percent of Facebook users were using their mobile phones to access the service.

Social networks are one of the main vehicles for content marketers to distribute their content. The nature of their interconnected network allows people to easily share and redistribute your content to their connections. These connections are what allow your content to distribute virally. There are many different social networks and each has its own unique audience and features.

Facebook

Facebook, which launched in 2004, is by far the largest of the social media websites by a factor of three and has over one billion active users worldwide. Users must register to use the site and create personal profiles. These types of personal profiles are to be used online by real people. Businesses must create separate pages to distribute their content (available at www.facebook.com/page) and can invite their customers and potential customers to "like" their page to get content updates. These content updates (wall posts) allow users to interact with you by posting comments (unless disabled.)

Here are a few tips to help get the most out of your Facebook page:

- Cover Photo – Your cover photo is the big photo on the top of your page which is the first thing your visitors will see. It should instantly convey your brand message and promise. Don't just choose some generic stock photo; spend time picking something that represents your brand and piques your visitors' interest so that they stick around.

- About Section – Here you can write a little about your company, including a URL, your location and more. Hint: be sure to include a www or http:// within your "short description" so that the link is clickable.

- Apps – Below your cover photo are usually four icons that link to other sections of your page. The first links to the "photos" you have posted on your Facebook timeline. The others can be for all sorts of different functions such as videos, content, e-commerce store, and more. You can include a total of 12 different apps on your page.

- Pinned Posts – Got something important going on? Want to make sure all your visitors know about it? You can "pin to top" and make sure that every visitor to your page will see your post. Pinned posts will appear on the top of your Facebook page for seven days.

- Highlight Post – Got a post that you want to stand out on your page? Hit the star button on top of that post and it will take up the entire width of your page.

- Milestones – Milestones are key moments you can decide to highlight on your page. Milestones are automatically expanded to widescreen and are visible to everyone visiting your page. You can edit milestones to add a story, photo, location, and more. You can use milestones to add personality to a page and tell a story.

EXAMPLE – Burt's Bees

With over one million fans, Burt's Bees handles their Facebook page and content marketing like a pro. Their page helps reinforce their brand identity, allows customers to share their love for the product, and tells you about their history. They also provide glimpses behind the scenes about their company's products.

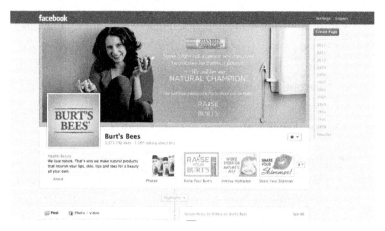

Twitter

This microblogging service is the second-largest social network. Twitter confuses people at little at first because it operates a bit differently from other sites. Users can send and read text-based messages of up to 140 characters, known as "tweets." Most tweets are public and users can follow anyone without needing to be approved.

Twitter has become a favorite avenue for content marketers. Barack Obama effectively used this new form of getting the message out during his presidential campaign, and everyone from magazines to movie stars uses it as a quick way to connect with an audience. By putting out a consistent stream of good content, you'll slowly find followers.

Here are some tips to increase your exposure and followers on Twitter:

- Follow people in your industry – Follow the present thought leaders in your industry and they might follow you back. It's a good idea to be connected to all the right people, even competitors.

- Connect through keywords – On Twitter keywords are called hashtags, and people use them to connect and maintain ongoing conversations regardless of whether they know each other. They can be used during shows, conferences, sporting events, locations, and common interests. Here are some examples #superbowl, #healthy, #contentmarketing. Hashtags have a "#" in front of the keyword.

- Manage your followers – Use a free tool like Manage Flitter to manage who you're following that aren't following you back.

- Leverage all your touch points – Make sure to put your Twitter link on all your existing marketing channels: Facebook, Google+, Pinterest, LinkedIn, and more. You should always try and cross-pollinate all your users to the outlets you're using. Also remember to add your Twitter name to your business cards, office or store front, shipping boxes, brochures—whatever gets in front of your customer.

- Sign up for Twitter Directories – Register for sites such as Twellow and Twiends. This helps people to find you better.

- Tweet frequently but leave room for engagement – Twitter is a little different from Facebook in that you can tweet more frequently and bother people, but you want to give people a chance to interact with your tweets. Experiment with your frequency and keep track of followers who drop off and those who retweet your tweets.

- Communicate – Twitter is a huge community that is open to communication with everyone. Ask questions and reply to others—be involved. You'll see that the more you engage with your audience, the more it will grow.

- Always provide value – Twitter is like all other media in that people aren't looking to get sold or preached to. You need to provide value in the content you share, either your own or that of others. Also, remember to keep it fun and try to focus on a small number of topics.

- Tweet at peak times – I once had a client that was a bit of a night owl on the West Coast of the U.S., and he would tweet things starting at 9 p.m. He was wondering why his page wasn't growing. He never thought that half of the U.S. was already getting ready for bed. Be aware of your business's peak hours and tweet then.

EXAMPLE – Sharpie

Yes, almost a quarter of a million people follow the Twitter page for Sharpie pens. They have an engaging conversational style that is fun and lighthearted. They never do a hard sell but encourage story telling about using Sharpie. Their community manager, Susan Wassel, says, "Everyone has a Sharpie story."

YouTube

YouTube is a video-sharing website which allows users to upload, view, and share videos. More video content is uploaded to YouTube in 60 days than the three major U.S. television networks created in their first 60 years. In 2013, YouTube averages 800 million monthly visitors and 4 billion hours of video viewed per month. In one single minute, a total of 72 hours of video is uploaded to YouTube; these numbers are staggering.

It's obvious that for content marketers, video is an amazing way to get your story across. If a picture is worth a thousand words, what's a video worth? From a business perspective, it's priceless. In today's fast-paced world, businesses have the ability through video to connect with their customers in a genuine way. Video has the power to create an emotional bond that other media cannot.

Here are a few tips for working with YouTube:

- Create compelling video – Not everyone is going to be able to create the next "keyboard cat" or "Charlie bit my finger." You also might not have the highest production value or the most viral subject matter, but what's most important is to have compelling video for YOUR audience. It should address their needs and wants and be engaging.

- Lighting – You might not be able to have the most expensive video equipment, but lighting is the most important aspect of video. Try filming outside or Google "3 point lighting" to get some idea about how to use lighting to your advantage.

- Make it easy to find – Google owns YouTube, which means it will be indexed by the number one search engine. You need to take a few things into account when uploading a video:

  ○ Title: Make sure your targeted relevant keywords are in the title of your video.

  ○ Description: Make sure you include your company URL in the description and as many keywords as possible that are relevant to your content and most likely to be searched.

  ○ Tags: YouTube allows you to add tags to all your videos. Make sure to use them; add your company name, domain name, and other relevant keywords.

- Create a Branded YouTube Channel – YouTube allows you to add your own branding and create your own channel. You can add a custom background, edit colors, create playlists, and more. Take advantage of having your own page on YouTube without the distractions of other videos.

- Add annotations to your video – YouTube allows you to add pop-up annotations within your videos with calls to action. They can be effective, but make sure to use them sparingly so that they don't take away from your content.

- Add a Post – Got news you want to share with your subscribers? Click on the feed and update your YouTube channel with your latest news and content.

- Cross-Promote: As always, mention your YouTube channel on all your other media outlets and cross-promote your channels and their content.

EXAMPLE – Michelle Phan

In 2007, Michelle Phan was turned down for a job at the Lancôme department store counter. She then started her own YouTube channel and has since become the number one YouTube "Beauty Guru." Phan's videos have been viewed over 600 million times, making her the number nineteen channel on YouTube with 2.2 million subscribers. In 2010, Phan became a spokesperson for Lancôme Paris and debuted her first jewelry line, Ever Eden.

LinkedIn

With over 175 million users, LinkedIn is the most popular social network for business people as well as one of the top social networks overall. It's also one of the most underutilized social networks by many marketers. LinkedIn is an amazing resource for B2B marketers and should be on everyone's radar. In 2013, the average household income for a LinkedIn user is $109,000, so you know these users mean business. For content marketers, LinkedIn allows you to share content and news both from your personal page as well as on a company page.

Here are a few tips to maximize your exposure on LinkedIn:

- Company Pages – If you haven't already done so, create a company page on LinkedIn. They allow you to share photos, documents, files, and job postings; to feature a group; to list your product and more.

- Add a Call to Action – LinkedIn allows you to add your products and services to your company page, including links to your website product pages. This is a great way to showcase your products and services, and it also helps out your company's SEO.

- Add Your Downloadable Brochures – LinkedIn allows you to add all types of files to your company page. Add your appropriate sales literature and other content to share with your followers.

- Create a LinkedIn group – Create a group about your industry or your company. Invite people to join and discuss things that are going on in the world. Make sure to add a link to any relevant groups you've created to your company page.

- Time your LinkedIn Updates – If you're going to share on LinkedIn, it's better to share in the morning or during normal business hours.

- Social Share Buttons – Almost all social networks have some sort of share button. Make sure to add them to your blog or anywhere you add your content.

EXAMPLE – ADOBE

Adobe, as one of the leaders in content creation tools, also knows how to do content marketing correctly for themselves. Their LinkedIn page has over 130,000 followers (which is a lot for LinkedIn) and they have beautiful pages that explain and link to all their products. They also have a great careers section that explains the benefits of working at Adobe.

Tumblr

Tumblr is similar to Twitter in many ways in that it updates the blog concept by making it extremely easy for someone to set up and share content. You can add audio, video, text, photos, social bookmarks, and even other people's blog posts on to your Tumblr with just a few clicks. It saves the time of uploading things to YouTube, Flickr, or creating a WordPress site. You can get started instantly and share media from your computer or mobile phone.

Tumblr users can follow other members and the posts of all the blogs they follow are combined and shown on their dashboard (similar to a Facebook wall.) Members have the ability to "like" your post or "reblog" your post to their Tumblr blog.

Tumblr has been growing very quickly and is the second-highest social network for engagement. Presently, Tumblr's user base is one of the youngest of all social networks and content presented should be short and sweet. Typically, B2C marketers have more success than B2B because of Tumblr's audience.

Here are a few tips to spread your content on Tumblr:

- Short-Length Content – Tumblr works best for images and a very short amount of text. If you have a very visual product, Tumblr is a natural fit.

- Lifestyle – Try and appeal to the lifestyles of your user. IBM features fun geek culture, and Tommy Hilfiger features "prep world." Think of what most appeals to your audience and have some fun with it.

- Follow, Like, and Reblog often – Listening and curating are key to engaging your followers. Use the search tool to find topics that match your brand's interest. You can also save your searches to quickly find topics of interest on a daily basis.

- Use Tags – People use tags to find your posts, so make sure to always include as many relevant tags as you can. Search and see what others in your industry are using as tags. You can also try and use an SEO keyword research tool to find common search terms.

- Google Analytics – Tumblr allows you to add Google analytics to your account so that you can monitor your web visitors.

- Custom Domain Name – You can use the default URL you are given or give your Tumblr a custom domain or sub-domain from your existing domain (e.g., tumblr.yourdomain.com).

- Add Comments – Tumblr does not directly support commenting, but you can easily add this feature by integrating a free tool from Disqus.com.

EXAMPLE – Kate Spade

Launched in 2011, Kate Spate engages with fans on a more visual level. "People are using and sharing beautiful visuals on Tumblr, posting things they think are inspirational," a spokesperson says. "In that vein, it seems like a really great platform for us to get our voice out there, not just as tweets and text, but through images and color, which is the DNA of the brand," she adds.

They interact with fans by frequently responding to and reblogging other users' questions and content. They also ask users to submit posts to them with their always present "Ask me anything" tab.

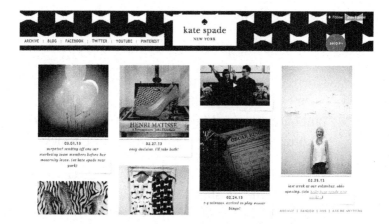

Pinterest

Pinterest is a virtual pinboard-style photo-sharing website that allows its users to create and manage theme-based image collections such as hobbies, events, different interests, and more. Users can browse other users' pinboards for inspiration, "repin" images to their own pinboards, and "like" photos.

People start pinboards on all sorts of topics to make it easy to remember where to find things. The all-time most popular pinboard categories are home & garden (17.2%), arts and crafts (12.4%), style/fashion (11.7%), and food (10.5%).

If you're selling goods online, Pinterest should be foremost on your radar. The ROI for Pinterest is one of the highest of the social networks. Its revenue per click is much higher than both Facebook and Twitter. Pinterest drives more referral traffic than YouTube, LinkedIn, and Google+, and its share is still growing quickly.

Here are a few tips to spread your content on Pinterest:

- Create your own business page – Visit http://business.pinterest.com/ to get your business pinboard started. Make sure not to use a personal account when you're pinning for your business.

- Beautiful Photos – Pinterest is a visual social network and it starts with great shots of your products. Make sure to always include links back to your website. If you're posting a picture of a particular product, make sure the URL you use goes to that specific product page. You never want your visitors to have to search around for any one specific product if they don't have to.

- Give your fans a voice – Encourage your customers to pin themselves using your product or service. Have them submit them and repin these photos.

- Keywords and Hashtags – Use appropriate keywords and hashtags in your descriptions.

- Curate Photos – Find other photos in your category that don't compete with your brand.

- Photo Alternatives – Infographics, charts, and text in images also work with Pinterest.

- Encourage Interaction – Ask questions and get your users engaged with your pins.

- Use Pingraphy.com - a scheduling tool for Pinterest posts.

EXAMPLE – la Madeleine

You might think that this French cafe's board would be all about French food but you would be mistaken. They cover a little bit of everything, from home décor, fashion, and weddings to even fun kid ideas. They have created a strong customer persona and pick things that identify with their customers.

Foursquare

Foursquare is a location-based social network that mostly runs on mobile devices, such as the iPhone. Over 30 million users "check in" using the Foursquare app on their phones at different locations. The app knows the user's location based on the GPS system that is integrated into most mobile phones. Users earn points or "badges" for checking into venues, and venues can also sponsor rewards such as coupons or free items for checking in. Foursquare is also available on the web.

Other similar location-based social networks exist but are usually tied in with other services such as Google+, Yelp, and Facebook Places. The main point for all content markers to remember for location-based services is that all information has immediate contextual relevance. Information should be short, clear, and concise.

Here are a few tips:

- Verify Your Listing – Check to see if your business is listed either on the web or using the mobile app. Ensure that all the business information is correct and complete. Make sure to claim your listing as the business owner.

- Local Updates – You can use local updates to talk to your loyal customers about anything new going on with your business. Updates can be anything—from news about an upcoming event to photos of the daily specials, and they show up right in your customers' friends tab when they're in the same city.

- Offer Incentives – Make your customers feel special by offering them specials for them to "check-in" at your venue. This helps build brand loyalty and people love to talk about rewards they receive.

- Give Insider Tips – People use services like Foursquare to get inside information about businesses, so provide it to them. Share your strength as a company and show the human side of your business. Give tips about your business and other businesses as well. Become part of your community!

- Create a Page – You can create your own page on their website. You can upload a banner and link your Twitter and Facebook accounts as well.

- Reward Your Mayor – People become the mayor by being local customers. Reward them for their loyalty and create a little competition.

EXAMPLE – Luke's Lobster Truck

One of my favorite lunchtime meals in NYC is Luke's Lobster. This multi-location restaurant saw a mobile need to service their customers throughout the city and opened up their food truck. They use tools like Foursquare to update their clientele about their present location, specials, tips, and more.

Google+

Google+ (sometimes written Google Plus) is Google's answer to social networking. It was launched in 2011 and has a total of 500 million registered users. Unlike conventional social networks like Facebook, Google has described Google+ as a "social layer" that isn't a single web property, but rather an all-encompassing "layer" that is connected to many of their properties.

People sometimes ask if Google+ is better or worse than Facebook. My answer to content marketers is that Google controls the most powerful search engine traffic source, so they should pay attention to the service. The benefits of search engine optimization cannot be understated, and I highly recommend you post your content to Google+.

Google+ functions pretty similarly to Facebook, but here are a few tips that will allow you to get the most out of the service:

- Hangouts Conferencing – Google+ allows for free video conferencing for up to 10 people. Use them to add a human side to your brand. You can conduct demos, classes, and more.

- Hangouts On Air – Allows you to stream video of live events to the web. You can stream keynotes from a conference, host a music concert, or moderate a discussion with experts in your field. After the event is complete, you can continue to share it via YouTube permanently.

- Social extensions for AdWords – Social extensions let people see your customers' recommendations by linking your Google+ page to your AdWords account.

- Google+ Pages in Search Results – When people search for your brand on Google, they can get the latest info straight from your Google+ page on the right-hand side of their search results.

- Google Authorship – Set yourself as an author with Google by going to: https://plus.google.com/ authorship

- This is the best way to get SEO benefits of Google+ for your content. Doing this allows the author's picture to show up to the right of a blog posts search listing, causing it to get higher rankings and click-through rates.

EXAMPLE – NASA

Believe it or not, this government organization knows how to do social media right. With almost half a million fans, NASA uses Google+ to spread information about their missions. You can join a hangout with an astronaut and see amazing photos from around the universe.

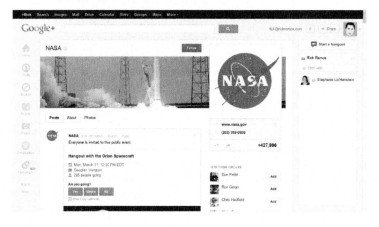

User-Generated Content

Creating a constant source of new content can be hard. It takes a lot of time to film video, write articles, go out and take photos, and more. The attraction to user-generated content is obvious. If done correctly, you can have users generate a mountain of content for you. This can end up being great content, but it's also amazing for SEO reasons as well.

User-generated content drives a bulk of the content on most of the top 10 web properties and is an integrated strategy for the rest of the sites. Looking at stats from comScore.com for early 2013, it shows Google, Yahoo, and Microsoft all taking the first three places due mainly to their search engines (content mostly supplied by others) with Facebook showing as the king of user-generated content in fourth place. Ask.com and Wikipedia, also on the top 10 list, are heavy user-content driven sites. Even Amazon and AOL, who depend on reviews and user comments, have a strong user-generated strategy.

Here's how big user-generated data is today:

- Facebook stores, accesses, and analyzes 30+ Petabytes of user-generated data.

- YouTube users upload 48 hours of new video every minute of the day.

- According to Twitter's own research in 2012, it sees roughly 175 million tweets every day and has more than 465 million accounts.

- 30 billion pieces of content are shared on

Facebook every month.

- The New York Times processes over 4 terabytes of images in 24 hours.

- The average Twitter user has tweeted 304 times.

- Over 5 million photos are uploaded to Instagram every day.

As you can see, the amount of content that is being produced by users every day is staggering. Getting users to submit and create content on your own site can sometimes be tricky and requires management, but the payouts can be big. Just remember, it's important to consider what makes sense for your type of products, your customer's typical behavior, and even your sales volume. You need to decide what works best for your industry and your specific company.

You should explore many different ways to get users to submit content to you. Here are just a few:

- Comments – Enable comments on your blog posts.

- Forums – Create a forum where your customers can talk about your product and share ideas.

- Guest Blogger – Invite just industry leaders or your entire customer base to share their stories on your blog.

- Product Reviews – Allow previous customers to rate your product either via text or video.

- Wikis – A wiki is a website which allows its users to add, modify, or delete its content; the most famous around is Wikipedia. Companies like Last.fm allow registered users to edit its music information to improve its data for everyone.

- User Photo and Video Submissions – Invite users to submit their photos and videos of themselves using your product to your site.

Here are a few tips to remember to get users to submit content on your site:

- Remove barriers – Users want instant gratification; make the submission process as simple as possible. Remove any barriers in your site design. Think about maybe implementing an optional Facebook one-click signup process to login.

- Motivate your user – Think about ways to encourage your users to submit content. Giving badges or other recognition can sometimes work. Offer a free product sample or monetary reward. Give a back link to their website to give them SEO benefits. Know your audience and tailor it to them but keep it fun.

- Respond – Encourage people to submit content by engaging with them in a timely manner. Set up alerts when possible to respond quickly to people.

- Allow them to share it – If your user has taken the time to create some content, give them a way to let their friends know. This makes it fun for the user and also gives you free traffic to your site.

- Community building – Building a community on a website is similar to a nightclub. No one wants to go to a big empty nightclub and start dancing in the middle alone. You need to start to build your community slowly and maybe seed some content.

- Open venues slowly – If you're starting something like a forum, don't start off with 20 different topics. Start off with one and expand as your user base grows. Having one lively topic is better than having 20 that don't get much traction.

EXAMPLE – Hotels By City

In 2009, Hotels By City launched an online campaign encouraging users to submit photos of themselves jumping on hotel beds. The idea was simple but users loved it and they even got national news coverage for the idea. Users were asked to go to BedJump.com and take a picture of themselves in mid-flight. It's funny and easy to do.

3 PR AND THIRD-PARTY PUBLICATION

The function of PR has changed in the world of social media, and it has an effect on content marketers. Pre-Internet, people would issue press releases and send them out via mail and fax to news publications. These communications were private between the news outlets and the companies issuing them. The PR cycle was very long, and it took a while for news stories to develop.

These days, many people use online wire services like PR Newswire to instantly distribute their news online to thousands of outlets. These press releases become instantly available to anyone. You can instantly issue breaking news direct to everyone without filers.

The SEO Press Releases

The idea behind a press release and its purpose has changed. Once you release your press release, it becomes public news, and people now find your news releases by using tools like Google News. Services like these work when people search for topics and news by keywords. This means the old press release now requires SEO optimization. When writing a press release, research SEO keywords to make sure you are optimizing your writing for the most popular terms in your field. Tools like WordTracker.com make this kind of research easier. Remember, you are using the press release as an inbound marketing technique to reach the public rather than pushing the news to news outlets.

Bylines

Have you ever read an article in print or online and thought to yourself, "I could write that"? Well, as a content marketer, you need to remember you can! You don't need to be a reporter to write for any publication. Newspapers, magazines, and websites are all dying for new content, and with increased pressure on margins, they are more open than ever to getting that content from experts in their fields for free.

Writing byline articles is one of the most effective tools you have as a content marketer to establish creditability with your target audience and become a thought leader. You can show your company as being in the know and ahead of the trends. Remember, all you have to do is ask the editors if they are open for bylines. It's usually better to reach out to them and see what kind of articles they are looking for, but I've known people who write an article and pitch it afterwards. It's easy these days to reach out to most editors via their website or though sites like LinkedIn.com. You can also check out HARO.com to become a source for a reporter.

Tastemakers

These days there are hundreds of thousands of blogs on

every single subject imaginable. Many times these small blogs have greater influence than larger magazines for some categories. The people that run these blogs become the tastemakers for their categories. Take something as simple as a sneaker, for example. Now, I personally I don't think about sneakers too much. I usually buy a simple pair of running shoes every six to nine months by going to the store and seeing what's available. This is in stark contrast with "SneakerHeads" that love all things sneakers. Sites like Sneakernews.com (believe it or not) are in the top 5,000 for websites in the U.S. So if you really want to influence the people that are most passionate about your product and if you want to have those people talk about you, doing blogger outreach is the way to go.

EXAMPLE – SneakerNews.com

Sneaker News is a daily report on the culture of sneakers published by Liquidrice, Inc. The site is read by over 3.8 million readers a month and has a strong influence over the most passionate sneakerheads.

4 SEARCH ENGINES

Search engines generally deliver an average of 50 percent of all web traffic to websites. Content marketers need to understand the volume of traffic that they generate and have a proper strategy when it comes to their content in relations to search engines. The good thing for content marketers is that creating quality content is the bulk of the work required for search engines. A few technical techniques are then all that's required to help the search engines discover your content.

SEO (Search Engine Optimization)

Many people think of secret "black hat" techniques and tricks when it comes to SEO, but while these tricks might work in the short run, they usually don't work in the long run and can seriously penalize your business. Google's main goal is to look for high quality content, and you need to do only a few things for it to stand out to the search engines. While a complete SEO strategy is beyond the scope of this book (but may be the topic of a future book,) I'll share a few simple tips to get you started:

- Keyword Research – This is the number one tip for content marketers. You should do keyword research for all content pieces before you even start writing—right after you pick the subject. Don't focus on very broad, single keywords like "dating" because these terms are incredibly hard to rank on; focus on "long-tail keywords" that are two or three words long. Once you have an idea for keywords, use a research tool like WordTracker.com to find more keywords. This is what you're looking for:

- Strong correlation to the subject you are writing about

- Relatively high level of search traffic

- Low competition from competitors

- Add an SEO plug-in to CMS – If you're using a content management system like WordPress for your blog (54.8% of all CMS's in 2013), make sure you add an SEO plug-in to help you manage your on-page SEO. This will actually take care of a lot of the hard work for you. Read their help files!

- Work in your keywords – When writing your headlines, titles, and page descriptions, make sure you try and work in your keywords but don't let readability suffer. Remember, your customers are number one, not Google.

- Analytics – Make sure you are running a tool like Google Analytics so that you can see what the most relevant pages are on your site and what searches are the ones that brought people to your site.

- Google Webmaster Tools – Google conducts 67 percent of all online searches, so it's a good idea to install Google Webmaster Tools to see how Google views your site.

Reputation Management

I've worked with many large websites that have woken up one morning to discover that their Google listings look horrible and might be affecting their business. Usually, this didn't happen overnight but was a slow process that no one noticed. The best way to combat this is… you guessed it, content marketing. Getting more listings into Google is as simple as creating more content everywhere and encouraging people to share it. Sign your business up for every social network that you can imagine, share things, do everything you've been reading in this book. Over time, your ranking will improve. Don't resort to tricks or short-term solutions that will have a long-term negative effect. It can take six months to a year sometimes to fully change a listing by SEO pros.

PART IV
CREATING
A CONTENT
STRATEGY

1 CONTENT AUDIT

Most companies don't have any idea how much content they are publishing on the Internet nor where it's all located. Content can live at tons of different locations: blogs, websites, social media sites, PDFs, PowerPoint documents, and much more. Before you can really plan for the future, you need to conduct a content audit to know your present situation. You need to figure out if your present content is relevant, up-to-date, and in the voice you want to portray. Here's a seven-step plan to conduct a content audit:

1. Conduct a content inventory – Your first task is to find and catalog all your existing content. This usually is easiest to do within a spreadsheet with each page labeled in its appropriate section. The level of detail you get into really depends on how much content you are cataloging and your business objectives. Some standard fields that people track are as follows:

   a. Page ID – You can establish a labeling system for all your content such as your home page being "0.0" and each subsection getting a different number identifier, such as "1.0." How you label it is many times affected by the size of your audit.

   a. Page Name – Just a general name for the site, such as "home," "product," "solutions," "services," "about us," etc.

a. Page Title – This is the title that the page is given that is displayed at the top of your web browser. This is defined within the source code of the page. If your pages are titled correctly, they will be clear and relevant titles that are rich in relevant keywords.

a. Page URL – Just copy and paste it from your browser into your document.

a. Page Description – It's usually good to create a simple description for your page for all your content.

2. Analyze your content – What is the subject of your content? Is it up-to-date with your present business situation? Is it accurate? Is any of your content out of date? Is it professional? Are style guides being followed? Is the same tone being followed throughout all your content?

3. Content Goal Review – Is your present content matching up with your present content marketing goals? Are your present and future customers being served by your existing content?

4. Analytics Review – Review your website analytics and see how much your content is being reviewed. Are certain parts of your customer service sections being reviewed disproportionally to other parts of your website? Are some pages getting next to no visitors? What search terms are people using to find your site? If you provide a search function on your site, what are the most popular terms? Is your site converting visitors into sales in expected areas?

5. Site Map Analysis – Is your present website structure functioning to present your content in the most efficient manner? Many times business needs change overtime, and an initial site structure no longer fits your needs. Review your site hierarchy and see if some content is in the wrong location.

6. SEO analysis – Is your content getting the most it could from SEO? Are you doing all the on-page SEO correctly with your page titles, descriptions, etc.? Have you done keyword research for all your content and added appropriate keywords? Are your keywords incorporated into your content?

7. Final Recommendations – Try and identify any missing pieces for your content strategy. Are you addressing your users' needs? Were any holes identified in your existing content? Is your site converting like it should be? Your final recommendation should be global and all encompassing.

2 CONTENT SCHEDULE

Think of yourself as a magazine or other content producer. Establishing a set content schedule enables you to think long-term about your content needs—those of your audience and your overall vision for content. Creating an editorial calendar is an old tool of the trade that helps you plan long-term for what content is needed and the subject matters you want to touch on.

One question my clients often ask is how much content should they produce. There really isn't an easy answer for this; it depends on your industry and organization. It's also dependent on what channels you plan on creating content for. For example, if you're sending out an e-mail newsletter, you might want to send them weekly or monthly. You don't want to inundate your registered users with too many e-mails. Look at your unsubscribe data, open rate, clicks, and sales, and try and find an optimal frequency to send your newsletter.

Long-form blog content can take a while to create while adding a funny photo to Facebook can take seconds. Try and create schedules for each separate distribution channel. Be creative but always try and remember your primary goal for creating this content.

When creating a schedule, try and also establish a formal breakdown on who within your organization will create, coordinate, and authorize all content. This will help create a clear understanding of accountability and establish a good structure.

EXAMPLE – The Wall Street Journal

THE WALL STREET JOURNAL.
Digital Network

WSJ Edit Calendar: 2013

NOVEMBER

Date	Event
11/1	Breeders Cup
11/4	Monthly Investing in Funds & ETFs (JR)
11/5	Energy (JR)
11/11	Wealth Management (JR)
11/18	Big Issues: Wealth Management (JR)
11/25	CEO Council Conference Issue (JR)
11/29	Black Friday Retail Shopping Coverage (SS)

DECEMBER

Date	Event
12/1*	Off Duty Holiday Gift Guide
12/2	Cyber Monday Retail Shopping Coverage (SS)
12/2	Small Business (JR)
12/5	Monthly Investing in Funds & ETFs (JR)
12/7	Pearl Harbor Remembrance Day
12/9	Encore: Planning and Living the New Retirement (JR)
12/10	Technology (Marketplace) (JR)
12/16	Wealth Management (JR)

They work from an editorial calendar a year in advance for major topics and refine their strategy as they get close.

3 RECYCLING CONTENT

It takes a long time to create content. There is no sense in creating great content to use it only once and never see it again. Recycling content makes it easier to supply all the different channels you have to fill on a daily basis. (Note: I'm using the term "recycle" and not "reuse." With recycling, you'll be taking existing content and adding to it to create something slightly new. For SEO reasons, you don't always want to reuse the same content everywhere; that's duplicate content and you can get a penalty for it.)

Here are tips for recycling content:

- Meetups – Hosting a meetup? Record the speakers and post the videos online. Take plenty of pictures and make sure to tag everyone.

- Training Material – Use an existing chapter from your training material as the basis of a blog post. Use slides from training and post them for everyone to see.

- Webinars – Record your webinar and slowly release short (two-minute) highlight clips.

- Twitter – Answer a question from Twitter in a blog post. Have an interesting Twitter conversation? Repost screenshots on your blog.

- Speech or keynote address – Write about your event

before it happens; make it the subject of a keynote. Record the speech and release it on YouTube. Get the audio and make that into a podcast. Release your handouts on slideshare.net.

- Interviews – Going to interview someone? Have it transcribed and release it as an e-book. Ask questions and release short question-and-answer videos. Follow up after an interview with answers to people's comments.

- Old blog post – Got an outdated blog post? Rewrite it with new stats and refresh the topic. Remember, don't repost old content or you'll get an SEO penalty.

- Other people's blogs – Someone wrote something you don't agree with? Write a rebuttal about their post (but remember to be nice!)

- Videos – Re-edit videos to make them into short (one-minute) videos. Take any TV commercial and put it online.

- Customer Service – Take customer comments and use them in a blog post. Take your customer service material and turn it into an article. Expand on a popular FAQ question.

EXAMPLE – The Alamo Drafthouse

The Alamo Drafthouse is a movie theater in Austin, Texas, that will kick you out if you send text messages while a movie is playing. A woman called the theater to express her displeasure with this rule after getting kicked out for using her phone. Alamo Drafthouse used this message as a backdrop for a "NO TEXTING" PSA that now runs in their theater—and it also has over 3 million views on YouTube.

4 ENGAGING WITH CUSTOMERS

Content marketing is as much about listening and responding as it is about creating content. God gave you two ears to listen with and two hands to write with. Make sure you use them in about that 50/50 ratio.

1. **Listen to Your Existing and Prospective Customers** – Try and identify your customers' social accounts and look to see what's important to them. Check out the kinds of content they share with others. Look to see if they are asking questions about you or your competition. If you can identify some pain points, you can try and address them within your content.

2. **Listen to Your Competitors** – Join your competitors' social pages either through your own account or a dummy account. (Facebook uses your likes to create ads, so you might not want to be seen liking a competitor's page.) See what kind of content they are creating. Identify the kind of content that is most shared with others. Check to see if your own content shows your differentiation from them.

3. **Discover Industry Trends** – Listen for industry terms and see what influencers are talking about. Compare that with industry trade publications or mainstream media. Sometimes you can identify trends before they go mainstream. Talk about these trends before others and cement your position as a

thought leader.

4. **Respond** – Get involved in the conversation; tweet back to people that have questions in your industry. Post a response on a forum to someone asking about your company. Engage with users and be genuine.

Use Google Alerts to monitor some specific keywords that are important to your company, such as company name, product names, competitor names, key executives, and more. You can also use a tool like Hootsuite.com to monitor Twitter for specific keywords. Additionally, you can use the search function on Twitter, Facebook Graph Search, Bing, and more to search for your keywords from time to time.

EXAMPLE – Rick Ramos

Even I have set up Google Alerts to watch for my own name to see when I get media coverage.

PART V
TOOLS &
TRICKS FOR
CONTENT
CREATION

1 HEADLINES THAT GET 1000% MORE CLICKS

Excited to read this section? Yes, you should be! The headline for this section is enticing and hopefully makes you want to read what's in this section. Headlines are the first impression someone will get from your article and are many times the teaser that will be used to share something on social media. Readers generally pay attention to the title for two seconds and quickly decide if they want to read an article. You need to catch their interest quickly. Here are the elements of a good, catchy title:

- Try and simplify your article to its core message.

- Create a hook that gets people's attention.

- Use your SEO keywords where possible.

So you might be asking, How do I create a good hook? Well, here are a few things you can try:

- Make the reader curious – Using words like "shocking" or "secrets revealed" always work. Try and think of other teaser words that work with your piece.

- Use numbers – "Increase your click-through rate over 5 times!"

- Ask a question – Address who, what, when, where, how and why. ("When to quit your job" or "Why your diet might be hurting you," for example.)

- Use the formula = Number (Reasons/Ways) (to/why) _____.

  Just fill in the formula and you can usually come up with a decent headline.

  ("5 reasons why content marketing works," for example.)

Just always try and make sure that your headlines match the content. Also try and keep a similar tone when possible on a headline. You don't want to be funny and cute with a headline when discussing something very serious in an article.

2 CMS

Content management systems (CMS) are the building blocks of many of the top websites on the Internet. They provide an easy way to update your website and blog without needing a programmer. They allow you to add to, edit, and manage your website. They work not only on managing your content but they also do a lot of behind-the-scenes work, such as:

- Generate navigational elements for a website

- Add search functions and site maps

- Keep track of users, permissions, and security

- Manage on-page SEO

- Allow plug-ins to extend features

By far, WordPress is the leading content management system. It's a great platform for beginners and comes with great documentation. Installation is pretty quick with a simple wizard and takes about five minutes. Updating to the latest version of the software is a one-click operation, and the software can be extended with a host of features by different plug-ins. WordPress comes with a simple WYSIWYG page editor, and it's pretty easy to figure out by playing around within the dashboard. For developers, it's programmed in PHP and has a good API that you can use to extend the features. WordPress also has an active community of people, which helps to make the system the leading platform in the business. Oh, did I mention that the software is also free?

There are other CMS systems available, and when speaking with your development staff or local technical support, there might be reasons to select another solution. All of them have their pluses and minuses. I've used several of them in the past, and all are pretty solid choices. Here's a list of the leading platforms:

- Drupal

- Joomla!

- ExpressionEngine

- TextPattern

- Radiant CMS

- Cushy CMS

- SilverStripe

- Alfresco

- TYPOlight

3 AUDIO/VIDEO TOOLS

You don't need to have a studio setup to create great audio or video podcasts, but a few important tools and tips will help you create better quality content.

Audio:

- Get a great mic – If your mic came with your computer or you bought it at Kmart, chances are it's not doing your content justice. A good microphone is directional, which means it captures sound directly in front of it and not everything in the room. A great mic can make your voice sound more pleasing than in real life.

- Pick the right location – You obviously want to record in a quiet space. If possible, you also want to record in a space without heavy echoes as well. Avoid rooms with flat, hard services like concrete floors, big glass windows, and conference tables. Rooms with heavy drapes, carpet, and big furniture absorb sound and minimize echoes.

- Use compression (limiter) – I'm not talking about compressing the file size but using a software filter that reduces the loud parts so that they are closer in volume to the softer parts. If you're doing any post-recording editing, this will make your podcast sound better. Google it!

- Use normalization – This is another software technique that you use after compression to boost the sound levels of your audio file to use the entire dynamic range of typical speakers. Once again—Google it.

Video:

- Upgrade your video camera – The video sensor in most built-in computer webcams is poor. Upgrading to an external computer camera can give you a better lens and bigger sensor. You can also take it a step farther and get a dedicated video camera, depending on your budget.

- Lighting – This can be more important than even your equipment. To start, make sure your room is well lit. Recording outdoors with natural light can look better than under indoor office fluorescence. Think about using professional three-point lighting techniques to really upgrade your video. Inexpensive LED video lighting is now available for under $25 per light; that can be a serious upgrade to your video production.

- Avoid using zoom – If you have someone filming you, make sure they aren't using the zoom too much. Also, as a general rule, avoid digital zooming features of any camera.

- Get a tripod – They give you more flexibility as to where you can shoot and they keep the camera steady.

4 ANALYTICS

It's become obvious that Google is putting a lot of emphasis on content since the beginning of 2013 in its search results. To track and evaluate your content marketing results, it is important to use analytics tools to measure your progress. You can learn which articles are receiving the most traffic and, more importantly, which ones are delivering the most conversions. While doing your analysis, you'll begin to see patterns and discover your sweet spot for content that delivers a strong balance of traffic and conversions.

There are many tools available to track your website's performance. Here are a few of the top ones:

Google Analytics – It's a free service that offers detailed statistics about your website and it is very robust. It's currently being used by over 50 percent of the top 10,000 websites on the Internet. I totally recommend you use it for your website as it does the majority of the work anyone would ever need. Google also offers a premium version of this software for enterprise customers.

Crazyegg.com – This is a great specialty tool that creates heat maps of your site. Heat maps are visual representations showing you where users click and what they do. It's a bit more advanced than the basic heat map that Google displays and can help you spot design issues with your site. Typically, you can use a tool like this for a month or two to try and identify any issues with your website.

Piwik – This is a free, downloadable, open source, real-time web analytics software program that you run on your own server. It provides you with reports on your site visitors, search engine and keyword information, and a list of your popular pages. Because of its open source nature, it can be customized by both plug-ins or in-house programmers.

SiteCatalyst (formally Omniture) – This Adobe product offers enterprise customers a large assortment of tools to analyze their websites. It has the ability to track and manage multiple sites with large data sets.

When using analytic tools, there are four main things you want to look for:

1. Engagement – Your main goal when developing content is to engage and entice a website visitor. When someone visits your site to check out your content, you don't want the visitor to glance at the content and quickly bounce off your site. If they are engaging with your content for longer periods of time, they are more likely to become customers.

2. Keyword Sources – Because SEO traffic is of huge importance to content marketers, you'll want to monitor what keywords are bringing users to your site. You'll want to see if they align with your marketing goals and see which words lead to the most conversions. You can also use these keywords in future articles and headlines to maximize your SEO traffic.

3. In-page analytics – Once the user gets to your site and reads an article, you'll want to see if they are converting on your website. You'll want to see

where they go and what they do after they have arrived. You can then verify that you have enough calls to action on your site driving the right results with your content marketing.

4. Social Shares – One of the great things about content marketing done right is the ability to have people share your content, but it's important for you to track these shares and see what content is the most effective. This can guide you in the future as to what gets shared the most and what gets you new customers. If you're using WordPress, a popular plug-in for a thorough analysis of your social activity is Socialmetricspro.com.

5 A/B TESTING

One of the great things about marketing on the Internet is that it's easy and inexpensive to constantly be testing new ideas and concepts. A/B testing, also known as "split testing," is one of the easy ways you can improve the content on your website and increase conversions. The basic premise is that you change a single item on a page and see if it has either a positive or negative effect on performance. For example, say you write two different headlines and don't know which one is going to resonate with your audience. You can do an A/B test between the two and see which one performs better.

Anything on a webpage can be tested: headlines, body copy, call to action buttons, colors, and page layouts. You can test a single change or multiple changes at once. One false rumor that comes up frequently is that A/B testing has a negative effect on SEO. Google actually encourages it.

One of the great things about A/B testing is that you can't deny the data. Many times in an organization you might have superiors that want to make a change to a website based on their "hunch." Because they're superior to you, you might feel obligated to make that change. With A/B testing, you can take the hunches from your website and work off real user data.

In my career, I've learned that great ideas can come from anyone. People come from different backgrounds and perspectives. I would encourage you to be continually running A/B tests on your important conversion pages and accept ideas from everyone.

Here are a few tools you can use to run A/B tests:

- VisualWebsiteOptimizer.com – It's an easy-to-use A/B testing platform that allows you to create different versions of your landing pages using a point-and-click editor; no HTML knowledge is needed.

- Optimizely.com – This is another A/B testing platform that has many fans of its low-cost and easy-to-use features. It's extremely easy to use and very intuitive. The user interface is very clean and beautiful. It's the one I prefer these days.

- Google Content Experiments – This free choice is good to use if you're on an extremely tight budget. It has a limited feature set and is not extremely intuitive, but I guess it's hard to beat free.

THANKS FOR READING.
NOW GO GET STARTED!

RICK RAMOS

WWW.RICKRAMOS.COM

RICK@RICKRAMOS.COM